Mirror Magic

Alex Ramsay

Illustrated by
Stuart Trotter

Evans

A mirror is made from glass which has a special shiny mixture put on to the back of it. That's why mirrors reflect things.

Hey look, when I lift my right arm, my reflection lifts its left arm!

Mirrors always reverse reflections. Right becomes left and left becomes right.

This writing is backwards.

If you hold it up to a mirror you will be able to read it!

That's because it curves inwards a little bit and reflects things larger than they really are. It's called a concave mirror.

Yes, mirrors that curve outwards do that.
They are called convex mirrors.

There's one of those at the shop. The shopkeeper uses it to spot shop-lifters.

You can use a spoon as a concave mirror. Look at yourself on the inside of the spoon.

I'm upside down!

That's because it's a very concave mirror.

Now look at the back of the spoon.
It's a convex mirror.

I'm a funny shape!

13

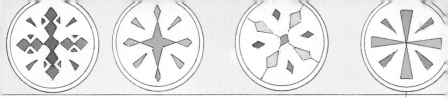

Inside a kaleidoscope there are tiny mirrors. Those lovely patterns are made by bits of coloured glass that have been reflected lots of times.

That mirror outside reflects the traffic on the main road.

It helps me to get out of our drive safely. It's a bit like being able to see around a corner.

Did you know that periscopes can be used to see around corners, too?

Yes, they have two mirrors inside them. They are used in submarines. Even if the submarine is underwater the captain can still see ships floating on the surface.

19

I'm using the mirror to see the cars
behind me. I can't turn around to look
because that would be dangerous.

21

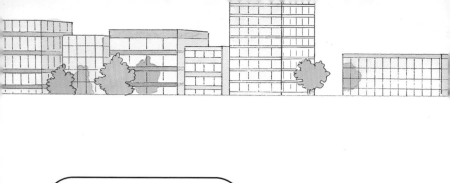

The glass on the windows acts like a giant mirror. It reflects the sky and the clouds.

I look tall and thin!

You look strange because all of these mirrors are curved. Only flat mirrors give proper reflections.

26

The water looks blue because it reflects the sky. That's why the sea looks blue on a fine day. When the sky is cloudy the sea looks grey.

27

Mirrors are useful, but they can
be fun, too.

Where would we be without mirrors?

Where would you find these mirrors? The answers are at the bottom of the page, but don't peep until you have tried yourself.

1.

2.

3.